MAX MORATH
ORIGINAL RAGS FOR PIANO

ISBN: 978-1-4234-5816-6

DISTRIBUTED BY

HAL•LEONARD®
CORPORATION
7777 W. BLUEMOUND RD. P.O. BOX 13819 MILWAUKEE, WI 53213

Visit Hal Leonard Online at
www.halleonard.com

MAX MORATH occupies a unique space as a spokesman for American life and music. As an entertainer and author he was prominent among those who spearheaded the Ragtime revival of the 1970's with his one-man shows in New York and on national tour. In a parallel career he has been a leader in the composition of new rags, rooted in the classic form of the early masters such as Scott Joplin, Joseph Lamb, and Eubie Blake. In his words, "These men set strict limits for rags: three or four complimentary themes of precise length, a duple time signature, the steady beat of a march delivered by the left hand — all of it adorned with the insistent syncopation that constitutes Ragtime's lure. At the same time," he says, "we composers of a later generation are challenged to blend the complex rhythmic patterns of the classics with the harmonic and lyrical innovations found since in jazz and musical theater."

A native of Colorado Springs, Max Morath worked his way through Colorado College as a radio announcer and jazz sideman, graduating with a B.A. in English.

Working in melodrama and summer stock theaters in the West, he developed an ongoing fascination with Ragtime and the dynamic America that spawned it. Graduate studies at Stanford's NBC Radio & Television Institute sharpened his media skills, and for PBS he wrote and performed two television series exploring the birth of ragtime and popular music. He was recently commissioned by National Public Radio to examine the broader area known as the "Golden Age of Popular Song" (1920-1960) and to write *The NPR Curious Listener's Guide to Popular Standards* (Putnam-Perigee, 2002). His frequent appearances as a pianist and guest on NPR have included "Piano Jazz," with Marian McPartland and the Wynton Marsalis series "Making the Music." He holds a Master's Degree in American Studies at Columbia University (1996), where his graduate thesis was devoted to the American songwriter Carrie Jacobs-Bond (1862-1946). He is soon to publish a book about her extraordinary career, and his essay "Ragtime Then and Now" is represented in *The Oxford Companion to Jazz* (Oxford, 2000).

"No one knows for sure," claims Morath, "where the word 'rag' came from. No matter. Today it has outgrown its misguided honky-tonk reputation and now, happily, joins those other essential and time-honored names for musical specifics: waltz and march, prelude and etude, minuet and mazurka, and now 'rag'."

*   *   *

Cover photographs by Diane Fay Skomars; music preparation by Tom Stewart (Echoes of the Rosebud) and Robert Marks (Three for Diane); All music BMI

RAGTIME, they say, "is a written form of piano music in duple time that surfaced around 1900, march-like in pattern, imposing syncopated figures in the right hand against a steady rhythm in the left."

This cool analysis may mollify the musicologists, but Ragtime itself was not cool. It was *hot*. Two young guys in 1900 said so in song:

> *"Got ragtime habits and I talk that way,*
> *Sleep in ragtime and I rag all day…"*

> Living a Ragtime Life
> Gene Jefferson & Bob Roberts

Gene and Bob seemed obsessed, as if by a force of nature. It happened to me too, about forty years later. My mother had stocked our piano bench with Scott Joplin and Zez Confrey and all the others in between. I mastered Joplin's *Original Rags*. Then I found his *Easy Winners* and James Scott's *Grace & Beauty*. These classic rags *had* to be played. Joplin called Ragtime "intoxicating." I found it addictive. Any kind of music can be played on a piano, but Ragtime *insists*.

It started life as a cultural outsider, its habitat the saloon and the sporting house. And it had this silly name, so it couldn't possibly be *music*. Out in the marketplace, though, professional musicians saw that this bonding of African rhythms and European harmonies would launch an irresistible new form. Many of us repeated the process when we discovered Ragtime years later. The place to play was again the saloon, or less clamorous settings like pizza parlors and road houses. So in the 1950's I was pounding hard-hammered upright pianos in noisy saloons, and my first rags lie in a Ragtime subset I'll call "loud & fast:" *Gold Bar Rag*, *Imperial Rag* and *The Vindicator Rag*. But I remember precisely the day I abandoned forever those sub-marginal uprights. It was at a concert somewhere in Indiana. Their upright piano was a miserable specimen. Offstage sat a Baldwin grand, a beauty. We rolled it out. *Easy Winners* had never sounded so good. I could sustain a *pianissimo*! I haven't played an upright piano since.

Abandoning the honky-tonk limits imposed on Ragtime sharpened my admiration for the music of Joplin and his contemporaries — Joseph Lamb, James Scott, and other early masters. Amid rich harmonies, their music juxtaposed syncopated inner voices in the treble against a relentless left hand. Joseph Lamb's work inspired one of my first efforts to compose for the grand piano rather than the saloon upright, when *One for Amelia*, dedicated to his widow, emerged unbidden from my fingers.

I don't know how the early Ragtime composers went about it, but I find that once you scribble down a rag's first theme and let it simmer for a few days, the other two or three strains come right along. The opening theme of *One for Norma* surfaced during a lonely late-night improvisation, obviously inspired by my first wife. On the other hand, *One for the Road* was composed through pure intention rather than inspiration. It's the title tune of "One for the Road," a musical I wrote and performed at the St. Louis Repertory Theatre in 1982.

Some of these rags were written against a deadline. *The New Black Eagle Buck* was commissioned by that fine New England band for inclusion in the E.B. Marks folio *Ragtime Current* (1977). *Echoes of the Cakewalk* made the first edition of the TRO/Hollis folio *Max Morath's Guide to Ragtime* (1964) as did *Polyragmic*, which I loaded with spiky syncopations and rampant time shifts. *Guide to Ragtime* also contained *Tribute to Joplin* — some of my favorite Joplin melodies revisited in a new medley.

Echoes of the Rosebud, recorded in 1975 for Vanguard, appears here in print for the first time — a salute to the old Rosebud Café in St. Louis, where Joplin and other masters met and played a hundred years ago. Two more editions of *Max Morath's Guide to Ragtime* came along in the early 1970's. I added *Golden Hours*, composed years earlier for Rudi Blesh, co-author of the essential history of this music, *They All Played Ragtime* (Knopf, 1950), and dedicated to his friend and co-author, Harriet Janis. *Three for Diane*, (1994), composed for my wife Diane Fay Skomars, is "three" in two ways: three-quarter time and in three sections, each based on one of our favorite songs. (Hint: Underlying that final theme is an eponymous pop hit from 1927.)

Among the early-day champions of Ragtime were the publishers John Stark & Sons in St. Louis and the Jos. W. Stern Company of New York. I count myself fortunate that my work has been published through the years by two of today's equally respected and long-standing firms: TRO (The Richmond Organization) and Carlin America — a company with roots in Ragtime's earliest years. The Jos. W. Stern Company was co-founded by Edward B. Marks, and did business under his name for many years. It was then acquired by Freddy Bienstock's Carlin America. One of their executives, Bob Golden, was first to insist that we undertake this Hal Leonard collection. E.B. Marks's editor emeritus Bernie Kalban also deserves special recognition and thanks here for his years of dedication to the publication of modern rags. Folios in the three editions from TRO couldn't have been produced so beautifully without the care and attention of Howie Richmond, the late Al Brackman, and today's TRO indispensable, Judy Bell.

The Cripple Creek story begins on page 40.

MAX MORATH

ONE FOR THE ROAD

Piano Solo

By
MAX MORATH

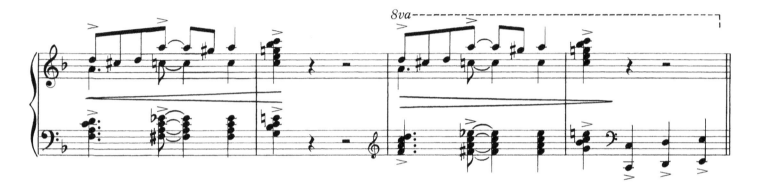

D.C. al Fine

Three For Diane

A Ragtime Waltz

MAX MORATH

59

64

Tempo I

69

74

79

Dedicated to the New Black Eagle Jazz Band

THE NEW BLACK EAGLE BUCK
(Rag for Band)

by MAX MORATH

Moderate March tempo

ONE FOR NORMA
(A Ragtime Intermezzo)

by MAX MORATH

rall. (Fine only) - Fine

8va

Tribute To Joplin

By MAX MORATH
Based on themes from rags by Scott Joplin

Traditional ragtime tempo *(not fast)*

One For Amelia

By MAX MORATH

Traditional ragtime tempo (*not fast*)

Polyragmic

By MAX MORATH

Bright ragtime tempo, well accented

8va bassa

Gold Bar Rag

By MAX MORATH

Bright ragtime tempo, well-accented

To the memory of Harriet Janis

Golden Hours

By MAX MORATH

ECHOES OF THE ROSEBUD
(RAGTIME VARIATIONS)
based in part on authentic Ragtime themes

by MAX MORATH

TEMPO I° (LIGHTLY)

A LITTLE FASTER

D.S. al FINE.

Echoes Of The Cakewalk

*(Authentic and Traditional Cakewalk Themes,
arranged and selected by Max Morath)*

Medium march tempo, with spirit

CRIPPLE CREEK
A Ragtime Suite for Piano

These six rags are dedicated to two 19th Century Americans, Bob Womack and Scott Joplin. Womack discovered gold in Cripple Creek, Colorado, while Joplin and others were staking claim to treasure of another kind in the new American music called Ragtime. Both men died broke as discoverers often do. Both changed the lives of a lot of people, mine included. The gold had lured my family west to Colorado, and filled my life with myths and stories when I was a kid. Ragtime set it all to music.

This Cripple Creek gold was no *easy* gold – not the pure and pretty stuff you could pick off the ground or pan from a creek bed. This gold demanded hard work in hardrock mines. It took labor and capital, railroads and machinery, money and muscle – all the elements of the bustling industrial society that marked America during the Ragtime Years.

Cripple Creek's mines opened in the early 1890's, when the Ragtime kids were breaking in their act at the Chicago World's Fair and every sporting district in the Midwest. Cripple's biggest year was 1899, the same year that Scott Joplin published the *Maple Leaf Rag* over in Sedalia, Missouri. So Cripple Creek's grand hotels and saloons and parlor houses had surely rattled with Ragtime for a few moneyed years. Never mind that water was rising in the deepest mines and the Great War was coming, when the miners would leave to dig more practical ores, and the Ragtime men, tired, would realize that the young fellows in New Orleans and Chicago were playing a new kind of music called Jazz.

The Ohio-born Morath brothers caught the gold fever upon news of the first strike – my grandfather Frederic August and my great-uncles Gene, Ed, and Charlie. Gene and Ed were cheerful, burly men who didn't mind physical labor if it led to a leasing deal on a mine or some shares in a town site hustle. They eventually followed new strikes west to Utah and Nevada, and settled into sunny retirement in southern California. Brainy Charlie Morath had tuberculosis, which they called consumption in the days when he died

young of it. But Charlie grabbed a small piece of Cripple Creek history. His signature, as secretary to one of the promoters of the Midland Terminal Railroad, can be found on the incorporation papers of that standard gauge link between Cripple and the outside world.

Grandfather Fred, far too fastidious to consider working in the mines, wangled himself a chair on the Cripple Creek Board of Trade and was soon dealing in real estate, where as we now know the real riches of Colorado lay waiting for the future. The Great Depression, alas, separated F.A. and succeeding Moraths from those acreages, and the Gold Camp years slipped into the family scrapbooks.

But Cripple Creek always seemed part of my life. For a kid growing up in Colorado Springs, the front range of the Rockies was a playground. The Old Stage Road and the Short Line roadbed to Cripple Creek were favorite hikes for me and my pals. At home, my mother Gladys Ramsell Morath, having lugged a piano bench full of Ragtime west from the family farm in Iowa, was playing rags and pop songs with rollicking accuracy on the parlor upright. So there I was, already getting the dual imprint of gold mines and Ragtime.

Then in 1948 I got a job playing the piano with a pick-up trio at Hammer's Tavern in Cripple Creek. It wasn't a ghost town by then, but it sure took high imagination to believe there had once been 60,000 people living there, with over three hundred working mines and two dozen trains in and out every day. Hammer's catered mainly to the few working miners still around, and some hardy townspeople who ran the county seat and looked after the ranchers in the high country. My job there lasted most of the summer, ending spectacularly one night when a 350-pound Welsh hardrock miner lifted one too many at Hammer's front bar and fell bottom-up into the bass drum. Angry words were exchanged, a Teller County deputy sheriff arrived, and my first Gold Camp gig rolled into history.

Not to worry. A few blocks up the street near Bennett Avenue the lights would soon be burning bright at the Imperial Hotel. Wayne and Dorothy Mackin, a young couple with more vision than money, had bought the old place. There would soon be action every night in the Gold Bar Room and Theatre. Cripple Creek would boom again!

Well, no. But in 1950 the Mackins founded the Imperial Players, and tourists began trickling in. I signed on as pianist and musical director, and proceeded to have the time of my life through most of the summer seasons in the 1950's. I composed the *Imperial Rag* for the 1954 season. It was my first try at an original rag and it bristles with Cripple Creek clamor. Two of the themes came to me while I was improvising chase music for the melodrama, "Hazel Kirke" or "Adrift from Her Father's Love."

On bright summer mornings in 10,000-foot-high Cripple Creek I took to hiking the old railroad right-of-ways to clear my mind and my lungs from the previous night's uproar and smoke. Dead mines and dying towns may be fascinating, I realized, but they are *ugly*. The Morath brothers and their kind had slashed the timber and scourged the hillsides, unhampered by environmental impact studies, but now, in the '50's, the aspen and pine were up strong again. The gold fever had given way to nature gracefully rearranging herself. The *Cripple Creek Suite* was simmering in the Colorado sunshine.

My walks often took me up to the Anchoria Leland mine at her stately location atop Gold Hill, looking down on the Camp. The very name was music to me. Anchoria Leland, I was sure, had been adored by some grizzled prospector — his wife or mother or baby daughter back East — tragically lost somehow, of course, before she could enjoy the wealth her namesake would produce. I tucked the name away along with a few musical fragments, but didn't finish the rag until 1980, at the welcome urging of the pianist Nurit Tilles, for her recording "Ragtime Here and Now."

The Vindicator mine you couldn't miss. Imposing as its name, it had always been a big pro-ducer and was still working during the 1950's. The name itself scans like a measure of Ragtime's 2/4 signature — VIN-di-CA-tor, jaunty and pugnacious. I never bothered to find out who originally located the Vindicator. I preferred the prospector of my imagination writing home, "They said I was crazy to leave home and hunt for gold, but I found it, boys, and there she is! The Vindicator!" It had grossed $27,000,000 so far.

There was a time when I'd have bet the Doctor Jackpot mine was named after a rag, not vice versa. It has that rough and ready, impudent quality of many of the early titles. I figured there had to be a Doctor Jackpot rag out there somewhere, but I checked it out and there wasn't. So now there is — named for the original's $3,000,000 gold jackpot. (And that's in those dear ancient dollars.)

Poverty Gulch was a favorite hike, the site of Bob Womack's fabulous strike, which he called the El Paso Discovery. He had sold the mine for a few quick dollars and ended his years in a poverty gulch of alcohol and loneliness down in Colorado Springs. The new owners renamed his mine the Gold King, which I never liked much because it seemed too literal and vain. But "Poverty Gulch," grim and gritty as it sounds, to me had a proud, quickstep quality, I suppose because I knew it had once held hope and then wild joy for Bob Womack. He couldn't read the future.

The Old Mortality mine came and went in the earliest days, and I never did locate what was left of it. But the name had triggered a bit of melody. It wanted to be a blues but wouldn't stay that way. I didn't go back to it until late summer in 1985, when word came of the death of Rudi Blesh on August 25th, a dear friend, and the co-author of *They All Played Ragtime* (Knopf, 1950), the book that inspired and informed the Ragtime rediscovery of the 1970's. Rudi was born in 1899, the year the *Maple Leaf Rag* was published and Cripple Creek gold production reached its highest point. So his name joins naturally with those earlier adventurers Bob Womack and Scott Joplin in the dedication of this Ragtime suite.

MAX MORATH

Doctor Jackpot

Max Morath

Old Mortality

(Slow Drag)

(Dedicated with Love & Respect to the Memory of Rudi Blesh)

Max Morath

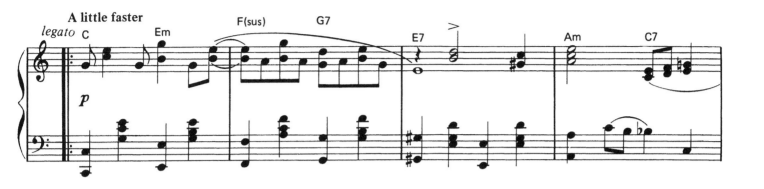

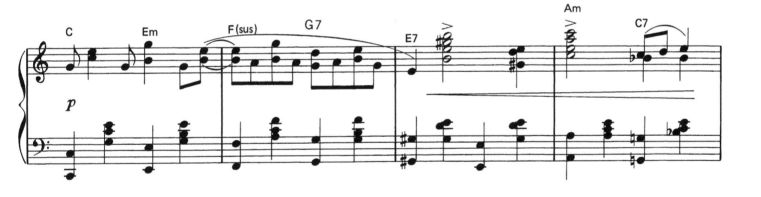

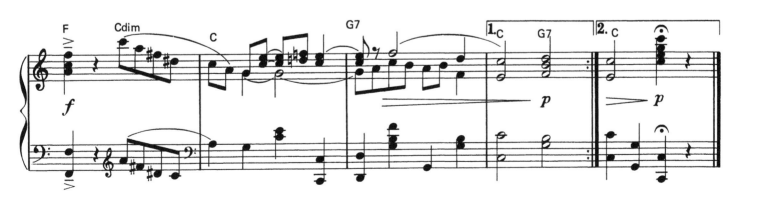

Poverty Gulch
(A Ragtime Two - Step)

Max Morath

51

52

The Vindicator Rag

Max Morath

D.S. al Fine

The Anchoria Leland
(A Rag)

Max Morath

Imperial Rag

Max Morath

Slow march tempo(♩ = 84 - 88)

D.S. al Fine